JAVA

PROGRAMMING GUIDE

SANDEEP BISHT

Contents

History of Java

The Birth of Computers

It was not long ago, well maybe around two decades, that there were still typewriters to create the documents we need at home, in school or for work. Remember your mother's recipes on index cards, your thesis in college, your resume for a job application and many more. Then here comes the birth of computer systems that made everything a whole lot easier! It was a total revolution when these miracle machines were introduced. Now, with just a click of the mouse or a keystroke you have photos printed out to decorate your home, a YouTube video of your high school ball, or a visually compelling marketing presentation for work.

A computer system consists of all the essential components of a computer and how they are integrated with one another for the device to function efficiently and effectively. Such components can be classified as hardware or software. Computer hardware pertains to the physical part, such as the central processing unit (CPU), mouse, keyboard and monitor, among others. Software, on the other hand, refers to the different programs that tell the computer what to do. Both hardware and software components work hand in hand to produce the user's desired results. Since this eBook was written to provide a step-by-step tutorial on Java programming, then we will emphasize on the software aspect of the computer system. In addition, the emergence of the World Wide Web or simply known as the Internet had brought forth more innovations in computer programming. The increasing demands of this online superhighway when it comes to sharing and communicating information has forced programmers to explore the potentials of JAVA programming language.

Evolution of Computer Programming Languages

* 1954-1957 John Backus with an IBM team developed FORTRAN (considered the first modern computer programming language but definitely not user-friendly).

* 1959 Grace Hopper at Remington Rand developed COBOL (Letter B stands for Business, which is COBOL's primary feature that included processing records of customers, employees and more)

* 1972 Dennis Ritchie at AT&T Bell Labs developed the C programming language.

* 1986 Bjarne Stroustrup at AT&T Bell Labs developed C++ that supported object-oriented programming (OOP).

* 1995 It was exactly on May 23 rd that Sun Microsystems released the first official version of Java programming language that is considered as an improvement of C++. This general-purpose software enables you to build and explore databases, write windowed applications and control handheld devices, among others. Just after five years, Java already had 2.5 million developers worldwide.

* 2000 The College Board announced in November that Computer Science Advanced Placement exams will be based on Java by 2003.

* 2002 Microsoft introduced C#, a new language named that inherited most of its programming features from Java. Sys-Con Media reported in June of the same year that there was an increasing demand for Java programmers (it has exceeded by 50% as compared to the demand for C++ programmers).

* 2007 Google started developing apps on Android mobile devices using the Java language.

* 2010 Oracle Corporation incorporated Java technology into the Oracle family by purchasing Sun Microsystems in January 2010 eWeek ranked Java in June as first among its "Top 10 Programming Languages to Keep You Employed" (www.eweek.com/c/a/ Application-Development/Top-10- Programming-Languagesto-Keep-You-Employed-719257). 2013 More than 1.1 billion desktop computers and 250 million mobile phones have been using Java platform since August 2013 (www.mobiledevicemanager.com/mobiledevicestatistics/250-million-android-devices-in-use and http://java.com/en/about). Moreover, Blu-ray devices emerged with more interactive capabilities through the new technology. Java was already considered the most popular language by various programming groups and communities, such as TIOBE Programming Community Index (www.tiobe.com/index.php/ content/ paperinfo/tpci) and PYPL that stands for the PopularitY of Programming Language Index (http://sites.google.com/ site/pydatalog/ pypl/PyPL-PopularitY-of-ProgrammingLanguage), among others.

Emergence of Java Technology

When IT experts realized in the early 1990s that there is a big demand in making people's lives less complicated by introducing intelligence to everyday home appliances, Sun Microsystems collaborated with a team of researchers to start the "Green Project". This is sort of a secretive assignment aimed to develop a portable home-appliance software that will run in embedded processor chips. The program should be flexible enough to adapt to the ever-changing appliance processor chips, which were getting smaller, cheaper and yet more powerful. The team planned to use C++ at first, but its portability issue was blocking their path to success. Thus, they decided to develop a whole new computer programming language.

It was in 1991 when Java language was initially conceived by Sun Microsystem through the collaboration of James Gosling, Chris Warth, Patrick Naughton, Mike Sheridan and Ed Frank. Oak was the initial name of the new programming language, which was the tree just outside James Gosling's window (the team's project leader). However, Oak was already being used as the name for another programming language. So in 1995 it was officially renamed to Java, which denotes the coffee that the software developers enjoy whenever they have their breaks. However, when the demand for such home-appliances did not turn out as what Sun Microsystem expected, the programming team has to find another channel to expand Java. Finally, in May 1995, Java was first released at the SunWorld Conference and was immediately followed by Netscape (the world's #1 browser at that time) announcing that they will incorporate the programming language in their development. With Java-embedded web pages, websites transformed from plain dull into interactive ones. Not only that the Web sends information to its audience, but they are also able to accept user input. In this chapter you have learned the history of computer programming languages, focusing on the development of Java technology. In the succeeding chapter, Java will be described on how it is used in various programming environments with a clear instruction on how to properly install it in your computer.

The Basics of Java Code

Before you start writing lines of Java code, this chapter will describe first what object-oriented programming is all about (which is one of the primary characteristics of Java programming). You will also encode your first simple Java program and understand the importance of every part. Also, you will be introduced to classes, objects and instances.

One must understand that the heart of Java language methodology is object-oriented programming (OOP). Over the years, software developers are progressively trying to find ways on how decrease the complexity of encoding programs. The first generation of programming languages involved toggling of binary machine codes, which are only a few hundred instructions long, into the computer's front panel. When programs evolved that required IT experts to handle more complex instructions through symbolic representations, then the assembly language was developed. As programming methodologies were enhanced, more high-level languages were introduced. One example is FORTRAN, however, codes were not easy-to-understand yet.

Structured programming emerged during the 1960s that was used in C and Pascal languages. These programs were characterized by local variables, rich control constructs and stand-alone subroutines, among others. Even if they were considered as power tools, they are still limited when handling very large projects.

The demand for breaking through the barriers of encoding extremely large projects paved way to the advent of object-oriented programming. It is a combination of the best methodologies of structured programming plus new organizing concepts. This programming style is characterized by the following:

*** Encapsulation**

By the name itself, encapsulation is a strategy that binds the programming code and the data it manipulates and keeps them safe from outside interference. When code and data are linked together, an object is created. This object contains code and data that are either private or public. A private code or data cannot be accessed by any program that exists outside the said object. When it is public, then the other parts of the program are able to access even if they are not within the object.

*** Polymorphism**

This concept is often described as creating a single interface for multiple methods. It means you design a generic interface to a group of related activities. It further reduces the complexity of the program by letting the same interface to be used to specify a general class of action. A clear analogy is the steering wheel. No matter what type of steering wheel, whether a manual steering or a power steering, as long as you know how it works then you can drive any type of car.

*** Inheritance**

This process involves one object acquiring the properties of another object, which supports the concept of hierarchical classification. To better explain this, imagine a red delicious watermelon which belongs to the classification watermelon. The watermelon is further part of the fruit class, which belongs to a larger class called food. The food class has certain qualities such as edible and nutritious, that is further applied to its subclass fruit. The fruit has certain qualities as well, such as juicy and sweet. Now for the watermelon, it also has attributes specific to it, such as a tropical vine-like plant. Now combining all these qualities makes a unique red delicious watermelon.

Object-oriented programming is characterized by the application and organization of classes, objects and instances. These are actually the components that make up a Java program and are interconnected with one another.

*** Class** - Considered as the highest group, class encompasses everything in objectoriented programming.

*** Object** - Specifications set by the classes are being applied to the objects that are not loaded into the computer's memory. They are also instances of a class that act as blueprints ready to be used when needed. Thus, one class can have any number of objects associated with it (can even have zero objects).

*** Instance** - Can be the same as objects since they describe an individual instantiation. To understand their relationship with one another, imagine that you are developing a computer program that will keep track of the students enrolling in a school. Each student has a distinctive feature – hair style, eye color, skin complexion, height, weight and many more. In your OOP program, each student is an object. Now, even if the students differ from one another, they share the same list of physical features. These attributes or characteristics need to be compiled into a master list, which we call a class.

First Simple Java Program

Let us try again to encode a short sample program by following these instructions:

1. Launch Eclipse. Click **FILE > NEW > JAVA PROJECT**. Name your new project as **EXAMPLE**.

2. Create a new **EXAMPLE** class. Click **FILE > NEW > CLASS >** Type **EXAMPLE** for the class name.

3. Enter, compile and run the program.

Encoding the Java program

In Java, a source file is called a compilation unit and the name that you give a source file is very important. By convention, the name of the main class should match the name of the file that holds the program. Take note that Java programming is case sensitive, which means the compiler distinguishes between lowercase and uppercase letters. Also, the filename extension required by the compiler is .java. Following this programming convention makes it easier to organize and keep track of your lines of code. Also, if you change the capitalization or the naming convention, then the whole program becomes meaningless and will stop working. So for this activity, we named it Example.java (since the public class defined by the program is also Example).

Compiling the Java Program

In this stage, the compiler javac is being executed and creates a file called Example.class that contains the bytecode version of the program. In the previous discussion, the bytecode is executed by the Java Virtual Machine. To actually run the program, use the Java interpreter called java by passing the class name Example as a command-line argument as shown below:

java Example

The following output is displayed when the program is run:

Java is essential to the Web

During compilation, each individual class is placed into its own output file named after the class with .class extension. It has been a convention to name your Java source file the same name as the class file so that when you execute the Java interpreter, you are actually specifying the name of the class that you want to be executed.

Parts of the Java Program

*** Comments**

Comments are the descriptive parts of the program that explain what the codes are all about. They are special sections of text that improve the program's readability - helping people understand the operation of the program. Basically, these are the words that we humans read but the compiler totally ignores. There are two types of comments, depending on how you write them:

1.One-Line or End-of-Line Comment

Starting with two slashes, this comment text is short enough to fit on one line. It is also written at the end of a line of code. In the previous simple Java program example, the oneline comment that we have is:

// A Java program begins with a call to main ().

Everything is ignored by the compiler starting from the first slash up to the end of the line.

2. Block or Multi-Line Comment

This type is characterized by multiple one-line comments (meaning, your comment text is too long to fit in one line). However, the two slashes are replaced with an opening "/*" at the start of the comment and ends with a closing "*/" (to save time in writing "//" for every line). Again, the compiler ignores everything between the two slashes. In the previous simple Java program example, we have:

/*

* This is a simple Java program

*

* Call this file Example.java

*/

Prologue is a version of a block comment that is placed at the top or very beginning of your programs. It contains important information about the code so that every programmer will be able to get an idea what the program is all about just by merely glancing at it. Usually, the prologue is enclosed in a box of asterisks and includes the following information: filename, programmer's name and program description. If we are to modify the block comment above, it will look like this:

/** Example.java * Felix & Khatz * * This is a simple program that displays "Java is essential to the Web" on your PC screen **

* **Class Heading**

We now move to the next line in our first simple Java program:

public class Example {

This program line is called the class heading or class declaration, which is composed of 4 parts – the 3 words and the open curly brace (actually the entire program is considered as a class). Let's discuss each one of them.

The first two words, **public** and **class** are what we call reserved words or keywords. Such words are used for a particular purpose as defined by the Java language. You cannot redefine or use them to mean something else, like making them as names for your program. Below is a list of the common keywords in Java language:

abstract	assert	boolean	break	Byte
case	catch	char	class	const
continue	default	do	double	else
enum	extends	final	finally	float
for	goto	if	implements	import
instanceof	int	interface	long	native
new	package	private	protected	public
return	short	static	strictfp	super
switch	synchronized	this	throw	throws
transient	try	void	volatile	while

Analyzing each word, class is a marker that signifies the start of the class or the beginning of the program. It also states that a new class is being defined. In our first simple program, Example is the name of the class. On the other hand, public is an access modifier that controls how the class is being accessed (in this case, the information can be accessed by all other classes). If it was set to private instead of public, then only the current class has the access to it. Finally, the open curly brace "{" indicates the beginning of the class and has a corresponding closing brace "}" at the end of the entire program. Always coming in pairs, braces identify groupings of code for both the programmer and the computer.

Main Method's Heading

After the class heading, the main method heading comes next. Method is a subroutine in Java language that is the line of code at which the program will begin executing. It is simply a list of things to do. In our example, the main method has the following form:

public static void main(String args[]) {

Again, public is an access modifier keyword, which indicates that everyone can access the main method. This also means that this can be accessed by the code outside the class in which it was defined or declared. Static, also another reserved word, denotes that the method can be accessed immediately. The third reserved word is void that signifies the main method returns nothing (in some programs it could return a value).

Any information that is needed to pass to a method is received by variables specified within the set of parentheses that follow the name of the method. These variables are also called parameters and in our example it is only (String args[]). The declared parameter named args represents the arguments that the main method takes. String is the argument's type that stores sequences of characters. The square brackets "[]" symbolizes that it is an array of objects of type strings. Even if there are no parameters required, you still need to indicate the empty parentheses.

* System.out.println

Based on our first simple Java program example, our main method contains the following line: System.out.println("Java is essential to the Web"); System.out.println is a programming code that gives instructions to the computer to print something out. Let us discuss every part of it. System refers to the computer and when it becomes System.out it pertains to the monitor, which is the output device of the computer system. The next word, println (read as "print line") is a built-in Java method that is in control of printing computer messages. Overall, the line of code is what it refers to as println method call. You simply call a method when you want to execute it. Please remember that the first letter of a method call is always in uppercase and the rest will be in lowercase.

The text enclosed in double quotation marks inside the parentheses is the message to be printed out to the screen. These double quotes are in charge of grouping the messages together. At the end of the line is a semi-colon that signifies the end of the method call or programming statement (it is like period in the normal English language). All programming statements to be executed in Java end with a semicolon. This chapter gave you a guide on how to start encoding using the Java programming language. You also have a better picture of what are the different parts of a simple program. In the next chapter, you will take programming to a higher level by incorpoorating what you call a user input.

CHAPTER THREE

User Input

In this chapter the concept of user input will be introduced and incorporated into your Java programming language.

Based from the first simple Java program that we discussed earlier, you were not being asked to provide any form of input for the code execution. The lines of code just displayed the message on the computer screen. In the real world, programming requires a stable communication between the user and the machine. In Java language, this is what we call Input/Output or I/O streams. In this scenario a two-way communication is created where the user provides an input for the computer to process and then produces an output in return.

Getting the User Input

There is a built-in class called Scanner in Java language to easily get the user input. What it does is it acquires information from the input stream, either from the keyboard or a file, and stores in a variable. However, the Scanner class is not part of the core Java language so you need to tell the compiler where to find it. For you to use this, you need to include this line of code at the top of your program, just after the prologue section:

import java.util.Scanner;

Because of the additional statement, the Scanner class is being imported from the java.util package. To call or execute this class in the program, you need to use the following statement:

Scanner InputVariableName = new Scanner(System.in);

Now, the imported class Scanner was called to initialize a variable called InputVariableName (you can change this name to whatever you like but make sure it is not a Java keyword). This is followed by the assignment operator "=" that is in turn followed by the programming code new Scanner(System.in);. This expression creates an object and commands the program to store the value of the user input to InputVariableName. Please take note of the coding convention in variable naming: first letter of the words are always capitalized.

For us to utilize the output stream to show you what you have typed into the program, we need to include the following print out statement:

System.out.println(InputVariableName.nextLine());

The method nextLine() is included here that will instruct the program to return a string value that was inserted into the current line. It also tells the program to wait until it finishes searching for an input, so the program will not advance until you type something and press the Enter key on the keyboard. Let us further modify the println method by including an additive operator:

System.out.println("You entered " + InputVariableName.nextLine());

At this point, the output statement contains a textual information that will be printed out together with the Scanner variable. The messages are combined using the additive operator "+" found inside the parentheses. Now, when the user provides an input, like for example "Johnny", then the program will display "You entered Johnny" on the computer screen.

From the program above, the message "What is your name?" is displayed to prompt you to enter your name. After you have typed your name and pressed enter (see the text in green located in the Console Section), the program will display your name after the words "You entered " on the screen. The introduction of user input as described on this chapter had presented Java environment as a two-way form of communication – between the software programmer and the computer. You, as the user, will provide information for the computer to process through the execution of the lines of Java code. The succeeding chapter will now introduce the concept of variable declaration.

CHAPTER FOUR

Variable Declaration

Previously, we declared a variable to contain a text user input. If you want to create more complex programs then you have to store values in variables. This chapter will now focus on declaring variables as part of your programming style.

Assigning what type of variable to be used is done in a declaration statement with the following syntax:

<type><list-of-variables-separated-by-commas>;

Examples: int rows, cols;

String companyName;

Again, a variable is a placeholder, the thing stored in it is a value and the kind of value that is stored in a variable is its type. Looking at the declaration statements above, the word at the left (int, String) specifies the type for the variable or variables at the right (rows, cols, companyName). By the way, a Java variable can hold only one type of value and its value can change during program execution. So in the examples above, rows and cols variables can hold only integers while the second declaration statement the companyName variable can hold only strings. Below are the basic variable types in Java language:

Type Name	Description	Range of Values
Whole Number Types		
int (Integer)	- simplest data type for handling numbers - no decimal points - not ideal for precision data	-2147483648 to 2147483647

	- default value is 0	
byte	- has the smallest range for number data type - contains an 8-bit signed 2s complement integer - default value is 0	-128 to 127
short	- contains 16-bit signed 2s integer - default value is 0	-32768 to 32767
long	- contains 64-bit signed 2s complement integer - default value is 0	-9223372036854775808 to 9223372036854775807
Decimal Number Types		
float	- contains 32-bit IEEE 754 numerical values - contains decimal points - default value is 0.0f	-3.4×10^{38} to 3.4×10^{38}

<table>
<tr><td>char</td><td>- accepts a single character as data

- default value is \u0000 (represents an empty space)</td><td>thousands of characters and symbols</td></tr>
<tr><td colspan="3">
Logical Type</td></tr>
<tr><td>boolean</td><td>- default value is False</td><td>True, False</td></tr>
</table>

Please take note of the following declaration statements for each variable type:
int AnyVariable; or int AnyVariable = 0;
byte AnyVariable; or byte AnyVariable = 0;
short AnyVariable; or short AnyVariable = 0;
long AnyVariable; or long AnyVariable = 0L;
float AnyVariable; or float AnyVariable = 0.0f;
double AnyVariable; or double AnyVariable = 0.0d;
String AnyVariable; or String AnyVariable = null;
char AnyVariable;
Boolean AnyVariable; or Boolean AnyVariable = false;
As you can notice, String and Boolean are in uppercase letters. This is because they are data types that happen to be a class names too. Therefore, in code and conventional text we will use uppercase S and B.

Previously our Example Java program accepts a string value from the user. This time, we will alter the code so it will ask the user to enter an integer data type. Let us say the program will display the user's age after entering it.

In the last programming line, we used nextInt() to instruct the program to save an integer data type. Other data types that we can also scan are nextByte(), nextShort(), nextLong(), nextFloat() and nextDouble().

If you need to create more complex operations in your programs that require using multiple input values, then it is better to save the user input and declare the variable. In this case, it is must that you already have an idea of what the data type of that variable should be.

Based on the new program code, the Scanner variable InputVariableName was first saved into MyVariableName and then was used to display the user-generated input to the screen. After you have learned the different variable types and how to properly declare them, you will now be able to create programs with additional functionalities and complexities. In the following chapter, another feature will be introduced which is the application of the Java language operator.

CHAPTER FIVE

Operators

This chapter will describe the available operators that you can add to your lines of code as you program more complex scenarios. Operators are mainly used to control, modify and compare data in a Java language environment.

Since the beginning of this book, we have already been using the equal sign (=) or the assignment operator, which works by assigning a compatible value into a variable. In addition, arithmetic operators are used to control the value that will be assigned to a variable. If you can remember the mathematical operators you have learned in school, they will be the same operators you will need to perform mathematical computation in Java programming. Gaining the knowledge on how to use operators is an important requirement. All you need to understand are the symbols for each operator and their functions.

Arithmetic Operators

These are the most basic form of operators apart from the assignment operator.
Additive Operator (+) – Returns the sum of two values
Subtractive Operator (-) – Returns the difference of two values
Multiplicative Operator (*) – Returns the product of two values
Divisive Operator (/) – Returns the quotient of two values
Remainder Operator (%) – Returns the remainder of two values being divided

Increment/Decrement Operators

These operators increase or decrease the value of the variable by 1.
Increment (++) - Increase the value by 1
Decrement (—) - Decrease the value by 1
They can also be used as a prefix or preincrement operator where "++" is placed before the variable. This means that 1 is added to the variable's value before it is being used in any other part of the program (the value will be

adjusted immediately when used). When "++" is placed after the variable then it becomes a postfix or postincrement operator. This time, 1 is added to the variable's value after the variable is used in any other part of the program (the value will be returned first before it is adjusted).

Example: MyVariableName = 23;

MyVariableName++; - returned value is still 23

++MyVariableName; - returned value is adjusted to 24

Logical Operators

These operators, also called comparison operators, permit a degree of flow control to your program by comparing two values or set specific conditions. A Boolean value can be returned, depending on the two values compared, that will determine whether a certain block of code will be executed or not. This is the most basic form of logic in a computer program.

Is Equal to (==) - Checks if two values are equal

Is Not Equal to (!=) - Checks if two values are not equal

Is Greater than (>) - Checks if the value to the left of the operator is greater than the value to its right

Is Less than (=) - Checks if the value to the left of the operator is greater than or equal to the value to its right

Is Less than or Equal (<=) - Checks if the value to the left of the operator is less than or equal to the value to its right

Logical AND (&&) - Checks if both values are true

Logical OR (||) - Checks if at least one of the values is true

Bit Wise Operators These operators manipulate variables at the bit level in a primitive yet fast way. Since they analyze binary numerals, which are the smallest unit of addressable memory, they process execution in the quickest way possible.

And (&) - A 2 equal-length binary operator that performs with the logic operator "AND" and multiplies both elements with bits

Not (~) - A unary operator that performs with the goal of logical negation and complements the binary value of ones

Or (|) - An operator that takes 2-bit patterns whose lengths are equal and performs with the logic operator "OR" (results are either 0 or 1)

Xor (^) - An operator that takes 2-bit patterns whose lengths are equal (results are expected to be defined with a similar digit)

Now that you have learned how to manipulate operators, you will be more adept in understanding and automating more complex Java programs. Another programming feature that will be introduced in the next chapter is flow control, which demonstrates nonsequential lines of codes.

CHAPTER SIX

Flow Control

This chapter will emphasize on a non-sequential method of Java programming. You will get acquainted with the if-then-else and different loop statements. With our previous simple program examples, we were oriented that a Java class is executed in one direction – from the topmost line of code up to the bottom, or what we call sequential programming. However, there will be cases that you will be required to write codes in a non-sequential fashion, especially for those more complicated scenarios. This is accomplished using logical and looping statements, so you can control the flow of your program to perform more complex functions.

If-Then-Else

This is the most basic flow control statement that uses logical operators to determine whether or not a specific condition is fulfilled. Let us add an if-then-else statement to our first simple java program that will display whether the user is a minor or not based on the age that he has provided. By the way, in this example, one is considered a minor if the age is below 18 years old.

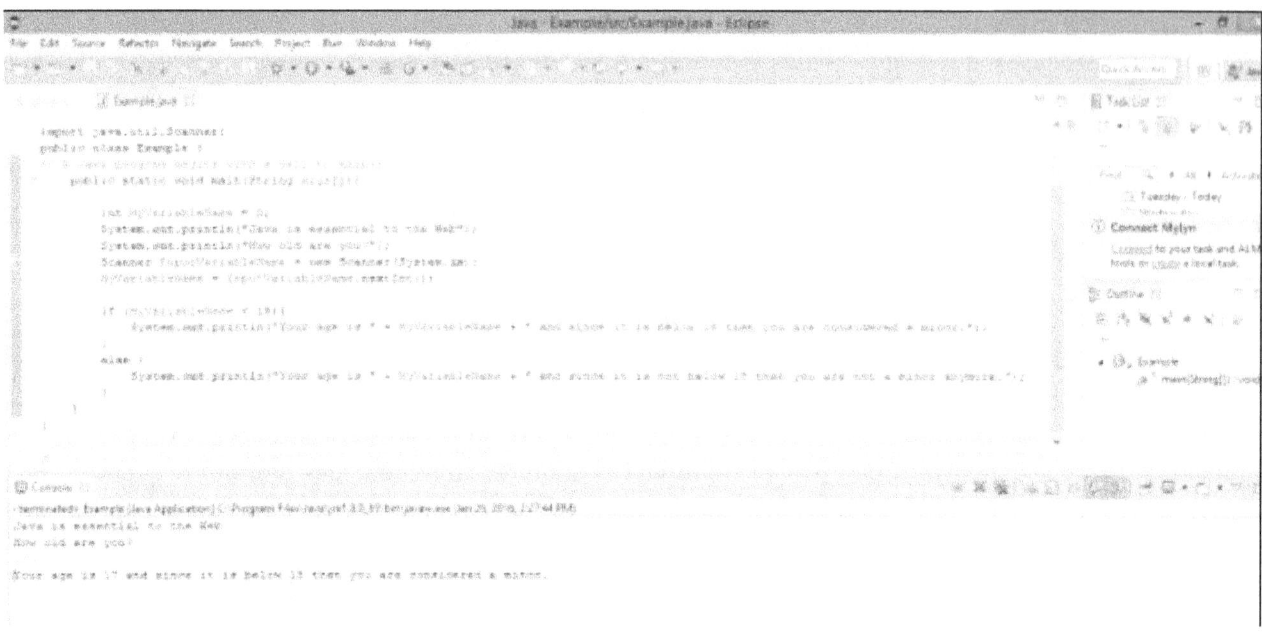

In this new set of programming codes, the condition tested is if the value of the user input MyVariableName provided is less than **18** or not. If it is, then the methods in the if block will be executed - displaying a message on the computer screen that the user is a minor (check the figure above). A block is also called a compound statement. Otherwise, the else block will be executed – notifying that the user is not a minor anymore (check the figure below). The else block is actually optional, meaning without its codes the program will just proceed to the rest of the class in case the condition is not met. Please take note that the parentheses around the condition and the braces surrounding the statements that are inside the if and else blocks, are all required. Also notice the indentation of the statements these symbols enclose.

Loops

This flow control statement allows methods to be executed over and over again as long as the specific conditions are met. In Java programming language, there are three kinds of loops that can perform repetitive tasks. We will also modify the simple program to do a countdown from 10 to 1 just to demonstrate the syntax for these loops. Again, do not forget the parentheses around the conditions, the braces and the indentations.

While loop – Considered as the simplest kind of "event driven" loop, this statement will execute the methods inside the while block as long as the specific conditions are met. Depending on the conditions set, this loop may never run even once.

In the program example above, the MyVariableName was first set to a value of 10. Next, the loop will check that while the variable is greater than 0, the program will display the value of the MyVariableName in every new line and then decrement it by 1. This will continue to run until MyVariableName is equal to 0. If at the start of program execution, the value of MyVariableName is already equal or less than 0, then the while loop will be bypassed.

Do-while loop – The main difference between this and a while loop is that the methods inside the do-while loop is sure to run at least once before the condition is checked. In contrast with the while loop, the do loop's condition is indicated at the bottom (this is the primary reason why the loop statement is executed at least one time)

In the program example above, again, the variable MyVariableName was first set to a value of 10. In the succeeding loop statement, no condition is checked yet. Instead, the do block will have to display the value of MyVariableName in every new line and then decrement it by 1 before the while condition is checked. This is what was discussed earlier that loop will definitely run once whether or not the conditions are met. Please take note of the semicolon at the right of the condition.

For loop – This statement is declared with specific parameters that control as to when or how many times the methods are to be executed. Variables that can be used to control the loop may be declared simultaneously within the loop itself. The form of the for loop statement is:

for (initialization; condition; iteration) statement;

The initialization part sets a loop control variable to an initial value. The condition is a Boolean expression that tests the loop control variable whether it is true or false. If the result of that test is true, then the execution of the for loop is continuously repeated. If it is false, then the loop stops.

In this final example, you will notice that all the parameters were set at the beginning, when the for loop statement was declared. So in the for loop declaration, MyVariableName was set to a value of 10, the condition whether it is greater than 0 is checked and then decrement its value by 1. After all these lines of code are performed or executed then the value of MyVariableName is displayed into the screen, each value on a separate line

In reality, there are usually a multitude of ways to accomplish a certain programming task. However, a good practice as a programmer is always to code your programs in an elegant way that entails choosing the most appropriate loop. One has the option to be creative and flexible, but this sometimes this leads to confusion. Through this chapter, you have realized that Java programming is not only onedirectional by integrating flow control through various looping statements. In the succeeding chapter, you will have a clearer image of what access modifiers are.

CHAPTER SEVEN

Access Modifiers

We have already been talking about Java variables, classes, fields and methods. Whenever they are declared you will have to indicate how they are controlled and how they are accessed in the entire program. Whether they are restricted or not, their accessibility feature will be determined by access modifiers that this chapter will take a closer look at.

Deciding on what modifier to use depends on your program's goal and what you are really trying to achieve. The following are the different types of modifiers:

Default

This is the type that is assigned when there is no access modifier specified. Due to its absence, any command or function can access a part of the program. However, its availability is only limited to access by fields that belong to a similar package. A program without a modifier can look effective but not quite clean. The level of access is usually open to the public but it is not included in an interface.

Example:
String version = " 1.00.1"
Boolean process_order () {
Return true
}

In this example, the program declared a string order version at the beginning. Since a specific type of access modifier is undefined, any command of function can be used to access the program component. Therefore, process_order can be modified easily.

Private

This is the type of modifier that accommodates the most restrictive fields in the program. It cannot be accessed, thus, cannot also be used by any command or function. Let's say a particular instruction is from an unlisted source, it cannot be granted recognition.

Example: public class arcadia extends bay {

private int name_of_residents

private boolean in_city

public arcadia () {

name_of_residents = joy

in_city = false

}

private void shrill ()

system.out.printIn (quiet);

public void action ()

system.out.printIn (talk);

}

For this example, the program defined a public class arcadia, which is allowed an extensive function bay. Although arcadia bay is set to public, some of its internal properties are set to private. In addition, since one of its internal components (action) is set to public, it can be acknowledged by different fields.

Public

This is the type of modifier that allows access from about any other field. With a public access level, it is less troublesome for a programmer to visit other parts of his work. All the commands, functions and different components of the program belonging to the public class can be accessed through a recognized set of instructions in Java programming language. However, being publicly declared has some drawbacks or limitations. Even if all the commands and functions are set to public, they cannot be accessed by classes that belong to a different package.

Example: public static void (string arguments) { }

Protected

This type of access modifier belongs to what we call a superclass and is characterized by being less hidden and secure as compared to the default type. It also signifies two things:

* it can only be accessed by the fields that are declared in a particular superclass
* it can only be accessed by the subclasses of a similar package

Such categorization is implemented to improve program structure while limiting the access of an irrelevant element. Protected access modifiers also impose strict protocols and the application is limited (cannot be applied to classes and interfaces). If a field is not connected to any class or interface, then it can declared as protected.

CHAPTER EIGHT

Classes and Objects

You have already been encountering Java classes and objects in the previous chapters of this eBook. At this point in time, you will gain more knowledge on the available class variables and objects that you can employ to achieve the desired results of why you are programming in a Java environment.

Classes

Acting as blueprints of a Java program, classes are templates that describe the characteristics of an element or method. Basically, they are generic elements in Java programming. They also help a programmer to understand the coding system of another programmer, making its structure clear. Classes exist in the program as long as they desire, meaning they do not have a lifespan.

The following is a list of possible class variables:

* **Class** - A class is a variable that needs to be declared before it enters a class, which can be found within any class and outside any method.

* **Instance** - Instance is a variable that remains within a particular class but is outside a method. However, it is accessible from any other method once declared.

* **Local** - A local is a variable that is defined inside any method in the program and requires initial declaration and acknowledgement. It is omitted after it has executed the command or function.

Objects

Java objects are elements that possess behaviors and states. When elements are defined, they come with their own features that further adds value to a program component without having to include an extensive feature. These are what you call instances of classes. Because of the behaviors and states of objects, methods are executed successfully. Furthermore, a particular object is associated with a unique function or command so it will adhere to certain instructions. In contrast with a class, an object ceases to exist once the program has been executed.

One of the characteristics of object-oriented programming is organizing things and concepts. There are three object relationships that defines why elements should or should not be moved to another particular program component:

* Is-a Relationship – this means that a type of object is more specific than its fellows (number 1 is a number)

* Has-a relationship – this means that a type of object contains or is associated with another object (given number 1 and number 2: number 1 has a succeeding number, number 2)

* Uses-a relationship – this means that a type of object will be using another object as a program progresses (given number 1, number 2 and number 3: number 1 uses a number 2 to arrive at the sum of number 3)

It is important that you know how to work around with classes and objects when programming using the Java language since they are considered as the generic elements of the software. You have also learned how they are organized and their existing relationships with one another. For the last but not the least chapter, you will be given an idea on what constructors are all about.

CHAPTER NINE

Constructors

One of the many Java concepts that this chapter introduces is the importance of constructors. Constructors are one of the many method-like things that allow the declaration of elements or the creation of new objects.

Constructors work as commands that need to match the other elements in a predefined function whenever they are invoked. They are also either defined or provided by default in Java programming language. Default constructors can set parameters but are not designed to carry out specific tasks nor perform unique actions. They cannot even take any argument. An explicit version of a constructor is required to allow the execution of particular commands and functions.

The main goal of constructors is to initialize the call to a fellow constructor by declaring special (). Upon the acknowledgement of a new constructor, a programmer is encouraged to create and set a parameter for the introduction of an object.

This

This constructor is used to pertain to a particular program component and most of the time it is used as reference to other constructors in a similar class, but in different parameter list.

Super

This constructor is usually identified in the first line of the programming code since Java compilers do not return a value if super is not declared initially. This keyword invokes a superclass constructor.